THE ANTIQUITIES OF
KING'S LYNN

From the Sketchbooks of the Rev. Edward Edwards

by

DAVID HIGGINS

PHOENIX PUBLICATIONS

ACKNOWLEDGMENTS

I would like to express my gratitude to the following organisations and people for their generous assistance and support: the staff of the King's Lynn Museums, especially Dr. Robin Hanley and Jill Walker; the staff of the Norfolk Record Office, especially Susan Maddock; the staff of the King's Lynn Library; Catherine Hall, Library Archivist, Corpus Christi College, Cambridge; Peter Sykes, David Pitcher, and Sophia Hankinson, who, as curator of the King's Lynn Museum in the 1960's, collected much material relating to the Edwards family. Finally I wish to thank my wife Brenda for her support and encouragement.

The King's Lynn Museums are part of the Norfolk Museum and Archaeology Service which, together with the Norfolk Record Office and the County Library Service, constitute the Norfolk County Council's Cultural Services Department.

The Illustrations in this book are subject to copyright and where not the property of the author are reproduced with the permission of the owners as follows:-

King's Lynn Museum IV, VIII, IX, XII, XX, XXI. 1, 2, 3, 4, 5, 6, 7, 8, 9, 11, 17, 18, 20, 21, 22, 24, 25, 28, 29, 30, 32, 33, 34, 35, 36, 37, 38, 39, 40, 41, 42, 43, 44. Front cover, Back cover.
Norfolk Record Office I, XI, XIII, 10, 15, 16, 19, 23, 26, 31.
King's Lynn Library V, VI, VII X, XIV, XVI, XVII, XVIII, XIX, 13, 14, 27.

Published in 2001 by Phoenix Publications
Walnut Farm, Beech Crescent, West Winch,
King's Lynn, Norfolk, PE33 0PZ.
Tel: 01553 840447

Origination and printing by
Clanpress, King's Lynn, Norfolk, PE30 2ND.

© David Higgins, 2001.

The moral right of the author has been asserted.

British Library Cataloguing in Publication Data
A catalogue record for this book is available from the British Library

ISBN 0-9540684-0-8

1. INTRODUCTION

For nearly sixty years, the Reverend Edward Edwards was a prominent and much respected figure in King's Lynn. When in March 1849 his funeral cortege set off from Tower House and made its mournful way towards St. Nicholas Chapel via St. James' Street, High Street, Tuesday Market Place, and St. Nicholas Street, shops closed, work stopped, and such were the crowds lining the route that it seemed as if the whole town had turned out to pay its respects. For Lynn it was nothing short of a state funeral.

The newspaper report of his death rightly drew attention to those qualities which had most benefited his flock. "We believe that he was one of the most liberal hearted men of the day......in him the poor found a ready friend and benefactor......Not a subscription list, which had for its object the benefit of the human family failed to secure his aid.......Not only did he give his money, but his services were as willingly rendered........that both in committees and on public occasions, no gathering together of our townsmen was considered complete unless he stood associated with them.....In everything that concerned the welfare of the town of Lynn, he always took a most lively interest, - and many of the institutions, useful and ornamental, are indebted to that good taste and sound judgment which he was ever ready to devote to the public service...... he was one of those men who through the whole course of his life walked undeviatingly on the crown of the road."[1.]

This then was the public face of the Reverend Edward Edwards, spiritual leader, friend of the poor, public benefactor, a model townsman who for these reasons alone deserves a place in the annals of Lynn. But in point of fact, it is to his private life we must turn to discover what it was that proved to be his most enduring legacy, especially for those interested in the town's history.

I   The Rev. Edward Edwards. Engraving by Wass after a painting by Samuel Lane. Published 25 October 1849.

Away from the pulpit, Edwards was a talented artist and historian with an enthusiasm for the relics of the past. Seeking a way to combine these interests, he produced a fascinating record, both drawn and written, of the town's ancient buildings.

It is an important body of work, for he features them as they appeared at a time when much was being demolished in the name of town improvement. It is special because, unlike his contemporaries, he recorded several actually in the throes of demolition, a response well ahead of its time.

The majority of the drawings originally formed the content of sketchbooks entitled 'Lynn Antiquities' and 'Scraps and Demolitions.' Each contained twenty wash drawings and a set of historical notes relating to the subjects depicted. Unfortunately some fifty years after Edwards's death, these sketchbooks were broken up, their contents dispersed and their original context lost.

Some of the drawings are well known and have been used to illustrate various publications. Fourteen from the 'Antiquities' series were published by Ronald Auker in 1977 under the title, 'Ancient Lynn by Edwards.' There have also been exhibitions featuring his work, most notably 'The Town Scene' in 1973. Now, for the first time in over a century, the material has been reassembled and can once more be appreciated as a whole.

In 1828 Edwards made the modest claim that his drawings had "afforded occasional amusement for upwards of twenty years." Could he have imagined that a hundred and seventy years later they would still have the power to do so?

2. THE REVEREND EDWARD EDWARDS M.A., F.S.A.

II Arms of John and Catherine Edwards, Terrington St. Clement Church

Edward Edwards was born on 2 February 1766 and baptised at Clenchwarton shortly afterwards. He was the son of John Edwards, gentleman, a marshland farmer, and Catherine, the daughter of Thomas Sommersby, a Lynn merchant and former town mayor.

His great-grandfather, Nicholas, was a Welsh drover who, on coming to Norfolk, married local girl Ann Dixon and settled at Islington. The church of St. Mary, Islington, is now in the care of The Churches Conservation Trust. In the chancel, fixed to the south wall, is a large ledger slab bearing the details: Nicholas Edwards, gentleman, died 3 December 1701, aged 42. Close by are memorials to various members of the Dixon family, local manorial lords, suggesting that if Nicholas was not already a man of means, he achieved wealth through   a 'good' marriage.

Nicholas's youngest son, John, was Edwards's grandfather. He was a man cut from a different cloth to his grandson, dying at the age of forty-nine "in consequence of his very irregular life."[2] This is a judgment borne out by his behaviour on the day before the birth of his own son John in 1778 when, "returning from Lynn Market (both at which & at Wisbech he usually staid 2 or 3 days & drank very hard) he fell (being intoxicated) into a Ditch from whence he was conveyd senseless to Mr. Forsters House (now R Rogers) at Clenchwarton & there restord to Life again."

The newborn John was Edwards's father. When he was nearly twenty-one he "had the good Fortune of meeting with a profitable Farm of £300 a year of the Countess of Portlands all rich marshland" Setting up home in the parsonage at Clenchwarton he asked his widowed mother to keep house for him. How, as a marshland farmer, he met and courted Catherine Sommersby is not recorded, but court her he did and on 10 January 1760 they were married in St. Nicholas Chapel, Lynn. The couple had six children before on 1st September 1779 Catherine died in childbirth. She was interred in the church at Terrington St. Clement but by then the young Edwards was already away at boarding school.

An Able Student

Edwards's formative years were spent in Clenchwarton, but he would have been a familiar sight in his grandfather Sommersby's house in the Tuesday Market Place (**39**), especially after his sixth birthday when he began his schooling "under Mr. Lloyd at Lynn."[3] By then David Lloyd had been master of the Lynn Grammar School for twelve years, operating from the   former Charnel Chapel of St. John (**17**).

After six years Edwards was sent to boarding school at North Walsham, to what is now the Paston College. He arrived at the same time as Joseph Hepworth, the new headmaster. He was clearly an able student, a boy the family could be proud of. Perhaps this is why in 1778 his father's cousin Francis singled him out for a legacy of £100.

On 1 July 1782, at the age of sixteen, Edwards became a pensioner of Trinity College, Cambridge, and began his residence there on 3 November the following year. This form of entry required him to pay for his maintenance and tuition fees, and aware that Corpus Christi awarded scholarships to students from Norfolk, he 'migrated' to that college in April 1784, although he had to wait a year to receive his scholarship.

At that time the Bachelor of Arts course at Cambridge was largely mathematical, but the more able students also studied the classics. Prizes were awarded for outstanding results. Corpus was a small college and not many students were contenders, although Edwards had one serious rival, a boy called Owen.

III Arms of Corpus Christi College, Cambridge.

Corpus awarded a prize called the Bishop of Lincoln's Cup. Owen received this in 1785, but a second cup, valued at £5, was presented to Edwards for outstanding achievement in the same examination. These events repeated themselves in 1786. In 1787 Edwards took his degree and, although he was second in the Class II (Senior Optimes) he was the best Corpus candidate and accordingly was awarded the Lincoln Cup.[4]

Being outstanding by Corpus standards, he was chosen as a fellow the following year. All the fellows were required to carry out one administrative duty in addition to their teaching responsibilities. Edwards began as steward, but soon became dean (of chapel), having been ordained deacon on 21 September 1788 and priest on 30 May 1790. He was now ready to return to Lynn.

The Evangelical Lecturer

In August 1791, the Rev. Charles Bagge, perpetual curate (vicar) of St. Margaret's, King's Lynn, died. The Rev. Stephen Allen, lecturer of the parish, was installed in his place leaving a vacancy for a lecturer.

The title of lecturer originated in the Commonwealth period, being bestowed by towns on unofficial clergy more to their taste than the official ones. In Lynn, by the late eighteenth century, the lecturer had become the priest appointed by the corporation to act more-or-less as a twin to the church - appointed perpetual curate. Between them they were responsible for officiating at St. Margaret's Church and St. Nicholas Chapel. The lecturer though was clearly the lesser of the two, for several of them were to succeed to the perpetual curacy.

Invariably in the eighteenth century the successful candidates for both posts came from Lynn's ruling merchant elite and fortunately for Edwards, by 1791, his own family, through their Sommersby kinship, had become part of that prestigious group. In 1777 or 1778 Thomas Sommersby, the younger, died without issue, leaving a substantial mercantile business to his sister's eldest son, Thomas Edwards, who had been apprenticed

IV The Rev. Edward Edwards. c1800
Portrait in oils. Artist unknown.

to the Sommersbys in 1774. In 1781 Thomas became a Freeman by virtue of completing his apprenticeship and was immediately made a common councillor. In 1784 Edwards's father John became a Freeman, by purchase, having made his first appearance in the poor rate books the previous year in relation to a substantial house in Chapel Street, which stood on what is now the Duke's Head hotel car park. He is soon recorded in partnership with a man called Danham, operating a small fleet of ships. It seems likely that he had been living in Lynn at least since 1775, the year he became a chapel warden of St. Nicholas. In 1788 Thomas Sommersby the elder died intestate. As a result Thomas Edwards added considerably to his mercantile business property and the Edwards grandchildren shared between them the sum of £5,000. Therefore at the time Edwards was seeking the lectureship, his father was a Lynn merchant and a chapel warden and his eldest brother was a merchant and common councillor. In addition, his uncle Nicholas was a surgeon and common councillor living in the Tuesday Market Place.

With such family connections and exemplary spiritual and academic qualifications, Edwards's application for the lectureship was little more than a formality. He applied for the post on 16 December 1791 and was appointed five days later, with a stipend of £100 per annum. On 1 January 1792 he preached his first sermon in the town and was to remain in the post a record fifty-seven years.

The lecturer was charged with preaching "at the Church and Chapel of the Parish of Saint Margaret alternately forenoon and Afternoon on every Sunday and on all festival and fast Days,"[5] but Edwards became more associated with St. Nicholas Chapel and is believed to be the last person to be buried there.

His style of Christianity was evangelical. John Dyker Thew, the proprietor of the Lynn Advertiser, recalled him

V   The Pulpit. St Margaret's Church, King's Lynn.

thus: "He used to walk to church in his gown, and, being a large and handsome man, his commanding presence was most striking. He was one of the old school of Evangelical Clergy; and he wrote a small volume upon the evidences of Christianity, which we published for him."[6.]

On 12 May 1808, Elizabeth, the wife of John Gurney, died. It was an event which was to start a lifelong friendship between Edwards and the Gurney family. Katherine Fry's book supplies the details: "The Reverend Edward Edwards of Lyme (sic) Regis was a great source of comfort and strength to the broken-hearted John, and to all the family that assembled in that stricken house. The tie then formed with the Reverend Edwards was most important in its consequences. It first made the Gurneys acquainted with the Evangelical portion of the Church of England, with which several of them, never Strict Quakers, afterwards united in religious communion. ....Mr. Edwards introduced family worship into our houses....."[7.]

They did in fact share more than a spiritual affinity; they had a common interest in drawing and the past. Edwards's published account of the Red Mount Chapel is illustrated by an engraving from a drawing by Rachel Gurney and in Katherine Fry's book there is a reproduction of a watercolour of Earlham Hall, copied by Katherine from an original drawn by Edwards in 1811. Rachel and her sisters had been taught to draw by John Crome, a leading Norwich school artist.

Daniel Gurney, Rachel's brother, a partner in the family banking business in Lynn, settled at North Runcton in 1816 and enjoyed a long and fruitful friendship with Edwards, eventually succeeding him as president of the Lynn Museum.

Although he became lecturer at a young age, Edwards was never to succeed to the perpetual curacy for the Rev. Stephen Allen did not die until Edwards was eighty-one. He did, however, acquire other livings. In 1799 he became rector of North Lynn St. Edmunds in relation to which in 1835 William White records him as "sometimes performing divine service in part of the oil mill."[8.] By 1841 he was an Honorary Canon of Norwich and in 1842 became vicar of East Winch. The same year, he celebrated his half century as lecturer by hosting a dinner for fifty aged people at his house and shortly afterwards he was presented with a silver waiter and a silver inkstand by the townsfolk in testimony to his long and valued service.[9.]

The Family Man

Shortly after taking up the lectureship Edwards accompanied a Mr. Venn to Hull and there was introduced to Miss Ann Pead. Three years and many letters later the couple were married at Sulcoates, near Hull. It is not known where they lived in the early years of their marriage. Edwards had available to him the lecturer's house, a grace and favour property which stood on the south side of St. Nicholas Street, against what is now Whites House, but it is possible they chose instead to live with his widowed father.

Their first child, Edward Pead, was born in 1798. John was to follow in 1799, and shortly afterwards Edwards bought a house in Tower Place from Henry Bell of Wallington. Bell had acquired it through his wife, Elizabeth, the only child and heiress of Scarlet Browne. It cost £1,600 (**VI**).

VI Tower House, Tower Place, King's Lynn. Home of Edward Edwards 1800-1849.

Further children arrived; Ann in 1800, Catherine 1802, George 1804, Maria 1805 and John Francis in 1810. Like their father, Edward Pead and John Francis were to enter the church, but the older boy's ministry was cut short by his untimely death at the age of twenty-three. George was to make a name for himself as an engineer, and was instrumental in the development of the standard diving dress.

In 1826 Edwards's wife died leaving three adult daughters to comfort their bereaved father. The first of these to marry was Ann. On 19 December 1827, in writing to his sister-in-law, Mary, the widow of his brother John, Edwards mentioned that he had had an approach for Ann's hand from the Rev. George Munford, a curate of St. Margaret's. With this letter we glimpse the writer's willingness to be guided by his heart rather than his head. Having laid the proposal before Ann, he tells Mary, "she seemed so far from being indifferent to him that I could do no less than return him a civil answer;. .... At the same time, old folks ought to have a little prudence; and I shall perhaps be blamed by some of my friends, for letting her marry a man without a shilling; for he has nothing but his curacy, and his friends are literally poor; as he has raised himself from nothing, entirely by his own exertions." He goes on to praise the qualities of the man he was to treat like a son.[10.] The wedding took place in 1828.

VII The Rev. Edward Edwards. Engraving by Bedwell. 1838.

Like most girls of her upbringing Ann had been taught to draw and, in 1833, at the request of her husband, she made a competent copy of her father's Lynn Antiquities sketchbook.[11.] Sadly a year later she was dead. George Munford was to remain close to Edwards. He too was interested in antiquarian matters and was to write books on Norfolk history and natural history. In 1845 he donated to the newly founded Lynn Museum a copy of Mackerel's History of Lynn, expanded by manuscript inserts, many copied from the commentaries in his father-in-law's sketchbooks. When in 1842 Edwards became vicar of East Winch, Munford was installed as his curate and in 1849 he succeeded to the living.

Another glimpse of Munford's relationship with Edwards comes from the letters of kinsman and poet Thomas Edwards Hankinson, also a Lynn curate. On 2 July 1832, in a letter to his brother Robert, he writes of a cholera outbreak in the town and his concern that "Mr. Edwards and Munford are going to Hunstanton, and I shall be left in charge of all the churches for a fortnight." On 5 July, he is writing to his father with the news that there has been fourteen funerals adding, "We sent for Munford back from Hunstanton. Poor fellow! from my heart I pity him."[12.]

By the end of July, the outbreak had abated and Edwards had returned from his country retreat in Hunstanton, the house he had had built in 1814, on the coast road, just before the sharp right hand turn into the main street of Old Hunstanton. That he was drawn to the place is shown by the fact that his daughter Ann was married there and in one of his sketchbooks there is a drawing of the chancel of the parish church.

John Francis was already the rector of Runcton Holme when in 1836 he married. In 1839 Maria married William Cox leaving Catherine to look after her father for the last decade of his life. Of all his children, Catherine seemed to be the one who cared for him most. The newspaper report of his death describes her as "His excellent daughter whose anxiety towards him was most unremitting....." It was not until after his death that she married, having devoted much of her forty-seven years to his welfare.[13.]

The Traveller

Edwards enjoyed travelling. It gave him the opportunity to pursue his interest in mediaeval ruins and his passion for drawing. His first recorded trip was to Oxford, with his father, in 1787. Later that same year, he visited York and toured Derbyshire. In August 1790, he travelled to France, staying in Paris until the 30th, having joined forces with a Mr. Ward and a Dr. Brooke of Dublin. Returning with them through Flanders and Holland, he landed at Great

Yarmouth on 22 September.

Significantly he had chosen to visit France little more than a year after the storming of the Bastille, while that country was still in the throes of revolution. It was to be the start of a pattern, for in July 1814 he was there again, shortly after the Emperor Napoleon had abdicated and yet again in the summer of 1830 (with his children Catherine, Maria and John Francis), at the very time a revolution was removing Charles X from the French throne.

VIII Travelling Home.

Edwards was an admirer of most things French including, it would seem, Bonaparte himself (he had a collection of medals depicting the emperor and a large replica of the Vendome Column, the monument to the Frenchman's victories, is prominently featured in his portrait by Delacour (**IX**)). His enthusiasm in this respect seemed to stem from support for the human rights ideals of liberty, egality, and fraternity which first shaped the French Revolution. These fitted well with his compassion for the less fortunate members of society. His daughter Maria shared his views. On 10 August 1830 she wrote from France to her sister Ann in the following terms: "It is really interesting to be in this country just now. The revolution is a glorious one & seems to have been carried on with much calmness & direction. There were certainly 5000 killed in the dreadful conflict here but liberty is gained & every one appears to rejoice in the changes - the people performed prodigies of valour, & everything now is perfectly quiet."[14.]

On the same visit Edwards shows us he was a mere mortal when, on anticipating his entry into France, he wrote: "It will be some comfort to hear something intelligible, after all the barbarous German that we have been lately assailed with," and "Well Englishmen come abroad to be puzzled and cheated and we endeavour to submit to it with the best grace we can."

Besides his trip to Hull, which has already been mentioned, he visited North Wales with Mr. Hankinson in 1805, Cornwall with Mr. Simeon in 1807, and Scotland with his children Edward and Ann in 1811. His last recorded trip was to North Devon, in 1838.

It is clear from the evidence of the 'Miscellaneous Drawings' sketchbook that he was active with his pencil on many of these occasions.

Institutions Useful and Ornamental

IX The Rev. Edward Edwards. Watercolour by Delacour, 1842

Edwards possessed considerable organisational ability and was ever willing to place this at the disposal of his fellow townsmen. In the nineteenth century, clergymen were expected to take the lead in welfare and cultural matters, but Edwards's involvement in these areas went well beyond the norm.

On the welfare front, he embraced any organisation which shared his religious beliefs, echoed his welfare aspirations, or gave support for educating the poor. He made donations to such organisations as the Society for the Relief of Poor Pious Clergymen, the Church Pastoral Aid Society, the Charity School for Girls in King's Lynn, and the West Norfolk and Lynn Hospital.

More directly he was secretary of the local branch of the Church Missionary Society and secretary of Lynn's Boys Charity School, from its foundation in 1808. The newspaper report of his death includes the comment that it was "an institution, we believe, of all others that most engrossed his attention" and "we were ourselves amongst those, who in our boyish days, sat on the scholars' form and had the privilege of receiving instruction at his hand."[15.]

His chairmanship of the committee for the Relief and Employment of the Poor in 1816-17 provides a link to the sketchbooks. In December 1816, he met a corporation committee to arrange a package of proposals to provide relief work. They included the demolition of a wall adjoining the south side of the Greyfriars Tower and the improvement of the walk from the South Gate to the North Sea Bank. This involved work in the area of the Seven Sisters, and from The Walks to Littleport Street (5). Shortly afterwards, the scope of the work was extended to include a footway through the east wing of the South Gate. (8)

His work as a King's Lynn Paving Commissioner illuminates his approach to the buildings he was drawing. The Commissioners' main purpose was to improve the functioning and amenity of the town by widening streets and bridges, removing obstructions and encroachments, paving streets and creating what is now London Road. They were most active between 1803 and 1816. As a Commissioner, Edwards was party to the decisions to demolish such structures as the Old Gannock Gate (7), the Ladybridge Chapel (20), and the Greyfriars Gate (29), but thinking as an historian he made a record of each one.

On the cultural side, he was able to further his antiquarian interests late in life by co-founding the Lynn and West Norfolk Ecclesiastical Architectural Society and the King's Lynn Museum, of which he was the first president. The society was founded in 1842 and the museum in 1844. It is fitting that the majority of his wash drawings now form part of the museum's collection.

In 1822, he was presented with the Freedom of the Borough in recognition of his services to the town.

The Antiquary

Edwards's interest in the buildings of the past largely focused on the mediaeval period. When writing of Heidelberg Castle, he commented: "It is rather too young a ruin for me having been built principally at the beginning of the 17th century....."[16.]

His tours were carefully planned to include as many ruins as possible, especially the remains of monasteries and castles which feature prominently in his surviving drawings.

On 11 December 1806, he was elected a Fellow of the Society of Antiquaries, as a "Gentleman conversant in the History and Antiquities of this Kingdom, highly deserving the honour....."[17.] One of his

X The Chapel at Houghton Le Dale, Norfolk. Engraving by Hay from a drawing by Edwards for The Beauties of England and Wales, 1809.

sponsors was the principal librarian to the University of Cambridge, suggesting that his antiquarian interests dated back at least to his university days.

The following year the antiquary and topographer John Britton (1771-1857) became a Fellow and shortly afterwards the two men struck up a friendship which was to result in some of Edwards's artistic and literary endeavours finding their way into print. Their principal period of co-operation was 1809 to 1812. Britton's view of the relationship is shown by the dedication he made to Edwards of a print of East Ba(r)sham House, Norfolk: "To the Revd E. Edwards M.A. and F.S.A. this plate is inscribed from motives of sincere esteem by his obliged friend. J. Britton."[18.]

Edwards's feelings can be deduced from the fact that the man shown in the interior of the Red Mount Chapel (23) is John Britton."

Britton and his partner William Brayley were responsible for a remarkable series of illustrated topographical volumes under the title 'The Beauties of England and Wales.' The first volume appeared in 1801 and the one which includes Norfolk in 1810. Edwards's drawing of the Greyfriars Tower (**XI**) was engraved to illustrate the King's Lynn section and another of his drawings, the Chapel at Houghton Le Dale was also engraved for the same volume (**X**).

As the publishers of the 'Beauties' wanted to restrict the number of illustrations, Britton decided to publish his own series, the 'Architectural Antiquities of Great Britain.' Edwards was invited to contribute accounts of St. Nicholas Chapel and the Red Mount Chapel to the third volume. Both pieces show him to be a competent and painstaking historian, sufficiently confident in his own abilities to describe an early history of the town as "Mackerell's pitiful history of Lynn."[19]

His involvement with the Red Mount Chapel went further than the writing of a descriptive history. By 1806 it was recognised that the building was in a dangerous state of repair and in 1808, in the mayoralty of his brother George, repairs were carried out to the fabric, especially the buttresses, and rubbish was removed from the interior. One can imagine Edwards discussing with his brother the desperate need for the work. It was only intended as a stop gap measure but, in fact, it had to suffice for a further twenty years. Full restoration did not take place until 1828-9 when Edwards, together with the Rev. Blencoe, raised a public subscription for the purpose. (**22**).

Like most nineteenth century antiquarians, Edwards was a collector. In his will, he makes reference to collections of corals, seals, shells, coins, medals, minerals and fossils, examples of which he had already donated to the King's Lynn museum.[20]

The Artist

XI Tower of the Grey Friars Monastery, Lynn. Pencil drawing by Edwards. 1808

To put it simply, Edwards was a talented amateur artist who between 1800 and 1833 produced a locally important body of antiquarian topographical work in pencil, and in wash.

He must have produced many pencil sketches of Lynn subjects, probably one for every wash finished piece, but only one, and tantalising references to a few others has been identified in the public collections.[21]

As he rarely signed his work, there is a good chance that some drawings remain to be rediscovered. The surviving pencil drawing, that of the Greyfriars Tower, the original prototype for the illustration in Britton's Beauties (**XIX**) and for the later wash version (**28**), displays a quality of draughtmanship and lightness of touch that suggests a measure of training. However, his wash work is of variable quality, perhaps reflecting the amount of time he had available to complete the original sketch. Most of his drawings in the Antiquities series are of a high standard; those from the Scraps and Demolitions less so.

If there is a weakness in his work it is his representation of people and animals. His figures are interesting in that they depict a variety of activities from the period, especially people at work, but they are relatively unsophisticated by comparison with other facets of his pictures. He was also capable of the occasional topographical mistake, such as the omission of a whole bay from his representation of St. George's Guildhall (**36**) and the erroneous attachment of the Old Grammar School to the north west corner of St. Margaret's (**17**). But in general terms the quality and accuracy of his output was as good and at times better than that of his topographical contemporaries.

His amateur status is self-evident, and he makes it clear that as an artist he aimed to entertain and amuse his friends, but the fact that a number of his drawings were engraved gives his work a certain degree of professional approval.

His earliest dated drawing, that of the back of the White Tower (**6**), bears the date Feb.19 1800 and in fact, (**2**) to (**7**) are all from 1800 or slightly earlier. At that time Edwards was thirty-four. His latest dated piece, the

Tailor's Arms, was drawn in 1833 when he was sixty-seven.

All his identified work is topographical and, moreover, largely of buildings, structures and ruins of the mediaeval period. It serves to tell us much about Edwards, the antiquary, and shows him to be ahead of his time in terms of his approach to the buildings of the past. In his day there was no real notion of conservation, little desire to preserve ancient buildings for their own sake, and yet Edwards was clearly aware of their significance. He was indeed an active paving commissioner playing his part in the decisions which resulted in the demolition of several of Lynn's mediaeval buildings, but he was there with his sketchbook, making a record. He is actually at the scene of the demolition of the East Gate (4), the White Tower (6), the Bellasis (9), the new Market Cross (38), and the house in King Street (42), vigorously drawing before there was nothing left. This is what makes Edwards and his drawings significant.

3. THE ANTIQUITIES OF KING'S LYNN

The material reproduced in this book is housed in three separate repositories: the King's Lynn Museum, the Norfolk Record Office, and the King's Lynn Library.[22] The background to this dispersal is somewhat complicated. In his will, following a number of specific bequests, Edwards made provision for "the remainder of my books, pictures, prints, and drawings.......to be equally divided among my dear children including Mr. Munford."[23] Unfortunately no detailed inventory of these items exists, but three sketchbooks and a collection of loose drawings were probably included. One of these sketchbooks remains largely intact and contains forty-two wash drawings, mainly of castles and monasteries from a wide area of England and Wales. The front cover bears the label 'MISCELLANEOUS DRAWINGS' and the flyleaves, "Catherine Edwards 1849"and "Drawings by EE from Original Sketches."[24]

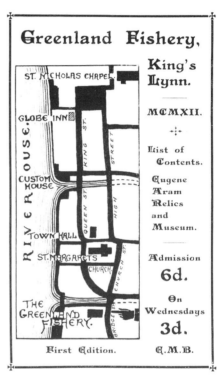

XII Guide to the Greenland Fishery Museum, King's Lynn.

The other two sketchbooks were devoted to Lynn topographical subjects. Each contained twenty wash drawings and a set of related historical notes (termed 'Brief Notices'). The earliest sketchbook, entitled Lynn Antiquities (or The Antiquities of Lynn) was, according to a statement written within it, completed in 1828.[25] The later sketchbook, called Scraps and Demolitions, was not finalised before 1833 as one of the drawings bears that date.[26]

Both Lynn sketchbooks became the property of Edwards's eldest surviving son George, for on his death in 1893 he bequeathed to his nephew, Stanley Edwards, a number of items "including my father's sketchbooks."[27] Shortly afterwards both were in the possession of E.M.Beloe the elder, as he makes plain in his book 'Our Borough : Our Churches.'[28]

Beloe died in 1907. Five years later his son and namesake founded the Greenland Fishery Museum in the Bridge Street building of that name. Featured in the displays were many of the drawings from the Lynn sketchbooks, but not

XIII The Lynn Antiquities sketchbook. Copy by Ann Munford, 1833.

all, for between 1894 and 1912 both were broken up. Beloe retained all the drawings from the Antiquities series, but transferred six, possibly seven, from the Scraps and Demolitions sketchbook, together with the covers and historical notes, to Harry Bradfer-Lawrence who seemingly wanted them to illustrate an historical work he was in the process of researching.[29]

The Greenland Fishery Museum suffered bomb damage in 1941 and the Edwards material was passed for safekeeping to the town museum. In 1967 the Bradfer-Lawrence collection including the other Edwards drawings, was deposited in the Norfolk Record Office. Shortly afterwards, some of this collection was transferred to King's Lynn, to the museum and the library.

This is probably how the two interior views of St. Margaret's Church (13)(14), which are not from either sketchbook, found their way into the library collection. In this process of dispersal, the Thoresby College drawing from the Scraps and Demolitions series became separated and its fate or whereabouts has not been determined.

Originally the historical notes were together on pages at the front of each sketchbook. Those from the Scraps and Demolitions sketchbook are now in the Norfolk Record Office, but there is no trace of their counterparts from the Antiquities. Fortunately Ann Munford's copy is also in the Norfolk Record Office. It bears the note "Copied for me by my dear wife in 1833 from drawings by her father, the Revd E. Edwards. (Signed) George Munford."[30.] It is not in fact an exact copy for Ann seems to have been unwilling to reproduce the section of the Red Mount Chapel (24) that Edwards had lovingly included, substituting for it an unfinished sketch of St. Margaret's Church, viewed from the south-west (10). The numbering in places is also slightly different. However, the historical notes are almost certainly a faithful copy of those in the original and in this work have been treated as such.

The original arrangement of the drawings in the two sketchbooks followed no discernible pattern and each included views of subjects covered by the other. In order to make the presentation of the material more coherent, the drawings have been arranged in this work under a series of thematic headings and a map of Lynn, contemporary with the drawings, has been used to show the location of the subjects depicted.

Each drawing is titled and captioned using Edwards's original words and at the end of most captions is a reference comprising the prefix LA for the Lynn Antiquities or SD for the Scraps and Demolitions together with the appropriate number from the sketchbooks. This will enable the reader to reconstruct the original arrangement should they wish to do so.

No attempt has been made to critically edit Edward's statements, although minor textual amendments have been made in the interests of clarity.

The sketchbooks were particularly light on depictions of St. Margaret's Church. This deficit has been rectified by including Ann Munford's west front sketch (10), the drawing of the Lantern, which is endorsed with notes in Edwards's hand (12) and the two internal views (13)(14). The lost Thoresby College drawing is represented by an alternative by Edward's friend William Taylor.

Finally a word on the reproduction of the drawings. Edwards worked in a mixture of black ink and ink watered down to produce a grey wash. Every care has been taken to create reproductions which are close as possible to the originals with the exception of that of the door in St. Nicholas Chapel (19), which Edwards produced in full colour and the Coney Brass (16), which he picked out in yellow.

A. FORTIFICATIONS

1. Kettle Mills

The round Tower was the northern extremity of the ancient walls, but very early (was) used as a reservoir for water. The name Kettle-mills is from the vessels employed which were formerly called Kettles. An entry in the Hall books in 1494 speaks of Kettle-mill and the kettles there, as kept by J. Bene. A windmill was erected here for raising the water in 1602 which was standing when Rastrick's map was made in 1730. (LA3)

2. The East Gate (Inner View)

It is figured in Carters Ancient Architecture as a specimen of English fortification, of the time of Edward III. It was repaired in 1541, and the arms of Henry VIII were then set up. The arch being very low, it was taken down in 1800 and the Kings arms were afterwards fixed in a wall on the North side of Littleport Street. (LA1)

3. The East Gate

The South side of this Gate was used as a public house, the "Hob in the Well." (LA2)

4. East Gates

Taken down 1800

The East Gates in a state of demolition. It was taken down in 1800, on account of the lowness of the inner arch, which would not permit a load of hay to pass under it. When the Houghton collection of Pictures was sold to the Empress of Russia and brought hither for embarkation they were stopped here and the waggons were obliged to be unloaded before they could pass. (SDI)

5. Town Wall with the White Tower

The walls, built before 1271, remained to this extent in the year 1800. The walk along the parapet passed through a room in the white tower, the floor of which suddenly giving way, an alarm was created, lest the whole should fall. It was therefore pulled down with all the southern portion of the wall. The ruins were formed into a terrace in 1817. (LA4)

6. Back of the White Tower

Feb 19 1800

Back of the White Tower Feb. 19. 1800

The other, or West side of this tower is also represented in the "Antiquities" and the reason assigned for its' demolition is there mentioned. (SDII)

7. The Old Gannock Gate

There seems to have been two Gannock gates; one stood at the end of the present mall and the other at the entrance of the chase. This was called the old Gannock and the drawing represents all that remained of it in 1800. It was taken down to lay at the bottom of the New road in 1803. (LA19)

8. The South Gate

The South Gate appears by the Hall books to have been built by Richd Hertanger, Mason, between the years 1437 and 1442. Henry Thorisby, Mayor. (LA20)

9. Fragment of a Bellasis or Outwork at South Gates

March 14 1827

For the use of the term "Bellasis" and its proper application to this fragment, see Parkin's History of Lynn, in his Continuation of Blomfield. But this building was evidently of a much later date than that to which he alludes. It was apparently intended to form part of an outwork, to guard the causeway from Hardwicke, during the civil wars and was probably never finished. (SDIII)

B. CHURCHES, CHAPELS AND COLLEGES

10. West Front of St. Margaret's Church

Drawing 7 from Ann Munford's copy of Edwards's Lynn Antiquities.

11. East End of St. Margaret's Church

The East end of St. Margaret's Church must have been erected after the time of Bishop Losinga. The building seen in the distance was part of the Benedictine priory to whom the church belonged. (LA7)

12. The Lantern

East Prospect of the Lantern of St. Margaret's Church Lynn taken down June 9 1742.

From Beloe's Our Borough: Our Churches

13. St Margaret's Church

The choir looking east (Loose Drawing)

14. St. Margaret's Church

The nave looking east towards the choir.
(Loose Drawing)

15. South Aisle of St. Margaret's Church

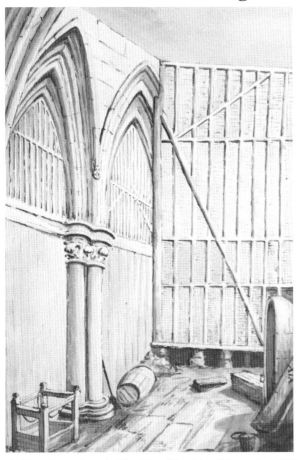

16. Gravestone of Walter Coney restored

This Tomb-stone of Walter Cony, one of the most distinguished among the ancient inhabitants of Lynn, is now lying in the Lumber-room, (under the floor of the present Library). But it formerly lay, where he was buried, in the Trinity Chapel, founded by him, on the North side of the Chancel, having been removed to make room for more modern gravestones. It was beautifully inlaid with his effigy and various inscriptions in brass. But these were stolen, broken to pieces, and sold to a brazier by one of the sextons, who being charged with his fault, and threatened with the loss of his place, hung himself in the belfry. An original rubbing by Gough of this Brass, is now in the British Museum. Seen by Mr. Bowskill. 1848. (SDXX)

A Chapel was founded by Thos Thorisby (Mayor in 1502) at the East-end of the South aisle of St. Margaret's church, dedicated to St. Stephen. Thorisby was afterwards buried there, under a handsome monument inlaid with brass, which being removed, and laid against the East-wall, the brass was torn away, and the whole destroyed when the present South Aisle was erected.
The East end being appropriated as a Vestry, the middle part was fitted up as a library, and the residue, towards the West, was used as a lumber-room, as represented in this sketch, and added to the Library A.D. 1834. (SDXIX)

17. The Old Grammar School formerly the Chapel of St. John

The Cupola (Though not remembered) is added upon the authority of Buck's & Bell's views of the town v. M.S. 1635

drawn partly from memory

This is called in Parkin "The Charnel Hall". And Mackerel says that in the year 1506 St. Margaret's church, being suspended, the christenings were performed in the Charnel, belonging to St. John's Chapel. (SDV)

18. Chapel of St. Nicholas

The present chapel of St. Nicholas was founded upon the site of one much more ancient, of which the tower alone remains. Parkin says the Pope's bull was granted to build this chapel in the Mayoralty of Jeffrey Talbooth 1374. But he occurs in the table of mayors 1371 & 1379. (LA13)

19. Door supposed to have belonged to a Confessional. St. Nicholas Chapel

This door is in the Vestry of St. Nicholas' Chapel. It had been white-washed, but was cleaned, and put into its present place by Mr. John Edwards when Chapel-warden. The standing figure seems to represent the Grand-Penitentiary and the words upon a label issuing from the mouth of a Priest at confession are very legible "Aperi michi portas justicie et confitebor Dno," alluding to Ps. 118.19. in the Vulgate. (SDXVIII)

20. Chapel of the Virgin at Ladybridge

The chapel of our Lady on the bridge appears to have been founded about 1329 by the same gild which erected that upon the Red Mount. The chapel gave the name of Lady Bridge to the bridge adjoining. Upon the dissolution it was bought (with other religious houses) by the corporation & sold by them Aug. 5. 1569. It was subsequently used as a dwelling house until taken down about 1806 to widen the west end of the lane called Stonegate. Sketch taken Aug. 3. 1803. (LA12)

21. The Red Mount, S.E.

The Gild of (Our) Lady (founded 3 Edw III 1329) seem to have had an ancient chapel here, as well as at Lady bridge, but the present elegant building was erected by licence from the corporation to Robert Cunance, Sept. 29 1482. The buttresses were repaired in 1808 and the stair cases etc. restored, & covered with a new roof, by subscription, in 1828. (LA5)

22. Wall surrounding the base of the Red Mount

A Subscription, amounting to more than £250, was raised in 1828, by the Rev. E.E. Blencoe and E Edwards, for repairing and restoring this unique and interesting building, when the Crypt, which had till then, been used as a stable, was cleared of rubbish, the original staircases replaced, the whole roofed in, mullions restored in the outer windows, and those of the Chapel glazed. Several excavations were made about the mount, which subsequently led to various improvements in the public Walks. It was found to have been formerly surrounded by a polygonal wall, of about eighteen sides, or faces, with buttresses at the angles and a Porch or entrance from the West, on a level with the lower Chantry or Crypt. But these were in such a decayed and ruinous state, that it was thought expedient to cover them in the following year. (SDVI & VII)

23. Crypt or Chantry of the Red Mount

opened 1828

*The figure introduced was
J Britton (pencil note)*

*A Section (upon a line drawn East
& West looking toward the South)
of the Lady's Mount or Red Mount
Lynn Regis, Norfolk 1809. (LA6)*

24. Section of Red Mount

25. The Workhouse formerly the Chapel of St. James

The Chapel of St. James was founded by William Turbe, Bp of Norwich, about the same time with that of St. Nicholas, in the reign of King Stephen, as a chapel of ease to St. Margarets. Part of it was taken down in 1547, and the remainder converted into a workhouse 1581. The governor and court of guardians were incorporated in 1683. (LA16)

26. Room in the Tower of St. James's Workhouse

The steeple over this tower was taken down in 1587. It now forms a bed-room. (SDXII)

27. Thorisby's College

Drawing By William Taylor. Text by Edwards

This was founded by Thos. Thorisby who was Mayor 1502 & intended as a College for Priests. The inscription still remaining upon the door seems to have begun with "Orate pro anima Majistri Thome Thorisby fundatoris hujus loci", the three first words being erased at the Reformation. It is here represented, as it must have been originally built, though many of the windows are now turned into modern sashes. In the beginning of the last century, it was inhabited by Edmund Rolfe Esq., for 35 years Town-clerk, afterwards Alderman & Mayor 1713. (SDIX)

C. FRIARIES

28. Tower of the Greyfriars Monastery

The Monastery of the Grey Friars or Franciscans was founded by Thomas Feltsham or de Foulsham about 1268. The Tower was supported after the dissolution as a sea mark by two strong buttresses, which seem by the inscription above them to have been erected in the mayoralty of John Percival, 1630. A house built under it was removed and the arches opened by Geo Edwards Esq in 1808. (LA8)

29. Gate of the Greyfriars

This gate-way stood at the N.W. corner of the precinct of the Monastery and, with a considerable portion of the north wall of it, was taken down to widen St. James St. in 1806. (LA9)

30. Gate of the Whitefriars

The Monastery of the White Friars or Carmalites probably (occupied) the whole field behind this gate now called the Friars in South Lynn. It was founded by Lord Bardolf in 1269. In 1604 Mr. Valinger, town Clk, had leave to dig stones out of the foundation of it to build his alms houses. The tower of it, which in 1612 was used as a dove house for the mayor, suddenly fell down, on April 29 1630. (LA10)

31. Gate of St. Augustine's Monastery

This is the only visible remnant of that which was once the most eminent Monastery in the town. In the year 1498 it gave lodging to King Henry VII, his Queen, the Prince, the Queen-mother, with many other persons of distinction. This Gate stands in the garden of Chas Goodwin Esq. The Prince was probably Arthur, eldest son of Henry VII. (SDXI)

32. Monastery of the Dominicans

The Monastery of the Black Friars, friars preachers or Dominicans, was founded by Thomas Gedney about 1268. It was enlarged in 1329; surrendered by the Prior and 11 brethren. (LA11)

D. ALMSHOUSES

33. Broad Street Almshouse

The Foundation of this Almshouse was laid June 1677 by Mr John Helcote a Tanner; who died before it was finished. It was afterwards endowed by Henry Framingham who Completed it the year following.

It is not necessary to add any thing to the dates Etc. recorded. (SDVIII)

34. The Bede House

The Bede or old Women's Alms house was founded in the 14th century by the gild of St. Giles and St. Julian, founded in 1384 or sooner. The house was built (or rebuilt) by Robert Soame, Alderman in 1482, by Thomas Soame, Mayor in 1636, and again by Benjamin Smith in 1822. It was enlarged in 1829. (LA17)

E. PUBLIC BUILDINGS

35. The Guild Hall

The Guild Hall was originally the hall of the Trinity gild called the great gild of the holy Trinity in Lenn, said to have been founded by King John. The rules and ordinances of which are given at length in Parkin. (LA14)

36. St. George's Hall

The Gild of St. George was founded by letters patent of Henry IV about 1408 and confirmed I Ed: IV. 1461. They had much property and a particular connection with the chapel of St. Nicholas. This hall has been successively used as a school, a sail makers loft, an exchange, a sessions house, a Theatre, and a wool warehouse. This sketch was taken June 7 1826. (LA15)

37. The Old Cross in the Tuesday Market Place

This is said to have been made in the year 1660 or 1661. (SDXIV)

38. The New Market Cross

Taken April 14 1831

This handsome building was begun in 1707 and finished in 1710 as appears by the following Inscription upon the frieze 'Porticus haec mundinaria, una cum macellis utrinque positis, et foro piscatorio a tergo, tam generosorum quorundam e comitatu, quam oppidanorum sumptibus, funditus extracta fuit, publico usui et ornamento. Dicatur hoc opus sub auspicies Car. Turner Praetoris, susceptum anno 1707, Johan Berney Praetore; finitum fuit 1710, Henrico Bell Architecto.'

By an account in the possession of the Town-clerk it cost £596.10s. But being built upon an arch, turned over a well on the East side, it settled unequally and ultimately leaned very much toward the West. The Cupola, being of wood, was suffered to fall into decay for want of paint and the whole building was taken down in 1831. The materials, being sold by auction in one lot were purchased by Sir. W.H.B. Folkes Bart for £160 and taken to his park at Hillington.

There were four Statues in the angles of this cross, representing the Cardinal Virtues, with appropriate mottoes subjoined; as under Justice, " suum cuique," Prudence, " nullum numen abest," Temperance, " ne quid nimis," Fortitude, " ne cede malis." (SDXV)

39. The Old Custom House and Mr. Sommersby's House

This was built upon the site of a former one in 1620. The King's "effigies" over it was that of James I. This was "new beautified" in 1667. The Market-place was then railed in, the timber being given by the Lord Townshend from his estate at Raynham. The four corner-posts were adorned with figures of the Lion and Unicorn. I have heard my Grand-father Mr. Sommersby say that he remembered, in the middle of this space a ring for bull-baiting. Copied from a very scarce Print by H. Bell. (SDXIII)

F. HOUSES AND HALLS

40. House in Bridge Street

Supposed (but without much authority) to have belonged to a Merchant of the name of Atkin. John Atkin was Mayor, in 1607 and 1615; William Atkin in 1619. The date 1605 is very visible in the North Gable, and 1674 on a corbel on the South. In 1834 some very rude paintings were discovered on the walls of one of the upper rooms, the largest representing the Parable of Dives & Lazarus. (SDX)

41. House supposed to have belonged to Walter Cony

Walter Cony was representive in parliament, four times mayor of the town, and fourteen years alderman of the Trinity guild. He built the trinity chapel on the north side of the chancel of St. Margaret's Church, where he was interred under a handsome tombstone inlaid with brass, which was removed when that chapel was taken down to widen the street in 1808. He died Septr. 14 1479, and this house was pulled down in 1816. The wooden carved posts at the corner were given to D. Gurney Esq. at Runcton and a carving of the town arms with a singular addition, which was under one of the windows, was affixed in the front of Mr. W. English's house in Church Street. (LA18)

42. House in King Street
taken down 1827

This house was at an entrance to a yard, called Linnock's yard and was said by some at the time of its demolition to be the oldest house in the town. The Bracket drawn was afterwards put up in C. Rising Church. (SDIV)

43. Ancient Hall now the Tailor's Arms Public House in Queen Street 1833

These are the poor remains of what appears to have been a large Hall, being about 66ft. long by 24 wide. nothing is at present known of its name or use. Could it have belonged to the Cell of Priests which Sir H. Spelman says (in Mackrell) was situated "near the Guild-Hall?", Or, might it not rather be the "Steward's Hall?". The Stewards of the Bishops of Norwich had formerly extensive jurisdiction here & held a Court every Monday in a place called "the High Steward's Hall," or "Monday Hall." (SDXVI & XVII)

44. Interior of the roof of the same Hall

4. COMMENTARY

Most of the subjects depicted by Edwards have been treated to historical examination in one publication or another and it is to these the reader must turn to discover more of their earlier history and, indeed, to check the veracity of his statements. A select bibliography has been provided to assist this process. The purpose of this commentary is to flesh out the contemporary context for the drawings and their subject matter and to outline the subsequent history of the latter.

A. FORTIFICATIONS

When Edwards took up the lectureship the town's ancient defences were still largely intact. They comprised an earthen bank pierced by gates, stretching from the South Gate to the Purfleet, just east of where St. John's Church now stands; a stone wall with gates and towers, which continued this line to the northern end of Kettlewell Lane; and a number of earthen outworks constructed between 1643 and 1645, during the English Civil War.

The Kettle Mills (1)

The picturesque Kettle Mills were a popular subject with artists and engravers. Edwards probably completed his original drawing in the first decade of the nineteenth century. Writing in 1857 William Armes commented, "The old (water) works of Lynn were simply a wooden tank in the old round tower, formerly one of the towers of the Town Wall, still standing but apparently doomed. The water was raised to this by an old-fashioned horse mill, and the pipes for the town were simply trunks of trees, bored upon the spot by the same horse power, and they were laid over the major part of the parish of St. Margaret's,.......Then the Water Works Bill..... was passed (1829). The tower and tank were erected, and the steam engine began to steam and smoke and growl upon the site of these former venerable works; and under ground the pipes of clay, which had displaced the wood, were themselves superseded by more hard and durable material, and we embarked upon the iron age."[31.]

Armes's fears were well founded. As part of the improvements to the works in the 1860's, the old tower was demolished. However, much of the town wall linking it to the Eastgate survives, albeit diminished both in height and character.

The town's first electricity generating station was established at the Kettle Mills in 1898 but in 1972 the site was cleared to make way for the single storey office building, now occupied by the King's Lynn Consortium of Internal Drainage Boards.

The East Gate (2)(3)(4)

The Eastgate controlled the road from Gaywood and central Norfolk, both defensively and commercially. The problem with the Houghton collection occurred in 1779 when George Walpole sold many of his grandfather's paintings to Catherine the Great, Empress of Russia for £40,550.

In May 1792, the corporation ordered that the arch on the east side of the gate should be taken down. If this work was carried out then (2) should pre-date that time, although this seems unlikely. In July 1800 the corporation ordered "that the East Gates and the Houses adjoining on the West and South Sides thereof respectively be taken down."[32.] Drawing (4) is a fascinating snapshot, sketched shortly after this order was carried out.

XIV Royal arms from the East Gate. Drawn by Farthing and etched by W. Taylor for The Antiquities of King's Lynn, 1844.

The high walls in (4) are in fact the projecting wing walls shown in front of the gate in (2). These were retained as bridge parapets and were not demolished until the turn of the nineteenth century when the reclaimed stone blocks were acquired by the then owner of Mill House, Tennyson Avenue (now a veterinary surgery) and used to construct boundary walls. Three of these stones bear inscriptions; EASTGATE EDWARD III, ...27-1377, and

AD1800, suggesting that shortly after the demolition of the gate, a commemorative record was cut into the surviving wing walls. The much travelled coat of arms, shown above the outer arch, in (2) is now set over the entrance to the Magistrates' Court in College Lane. It was placed there in 1982.

Of the structures depicted in the three drawings, only the nearest gate pillar, shown on the left of (3), survives, although the mediaeval bridge can still be seen beneath the modern one.

Edwards makes it clear that the southern rooms of the gatehouse were occupied by the Hob-in-the-Well public house and (3) shows a hanging sign and a man with a tankard to reinforce the point. In September 1800 the remaining portion of the land on which the Hob-in-the-Well had stood was leased to the brewer Edward Everard on condition that he built "a New House in the room of the old one lately taken down."[33]. The present public house of that name is the outcome. The name was taken from the play 'Flora, or Hob-in-Well' adapted in 1768 from an earlier play called "Hob, or the Country Wake."

The White Tower and Town Wall (5)(6)

The stretch of wall depicted in (5) ran from Coburg Street to the north side of St. John's Walk (the Red Mount Chapel can be seen in the distance). Edwards's notes give the impression that the whole stretch was demolished in 1800, but Armes, who was born in 1804, recalled that, "Within my memory,........much of Mr. Edwards' sketch remained, and every afternoon at four, when the schools discharged the boys, they might be seen in troops running along the parapet or playing 'hide and seek' in among the arches." He also wrote that "For years a considerable portion was made use of by the corporation rope makers, as they were generally called, and at length the locomotive of the 'East Anglian army' made an irreparable breach in the walls,........."[34].

It is a little surprising that Edwards was not more precise for, as Chairman of the Committee for the Relief and Employment of the Poor, the body that carried out the work, he was in a prime position to know the facts. The idea was to improve the public walk, then passing through the rope walk, by moving it to the outside of the remains of the town wall as far as the site of the White Tower. Beyond there, to Littleport Street, the wall was still intact but it was decided to reduce the width of this section by removing the walkway arches, thereby producing the degraded appearance the wall has today.

The archway shown on (6) is probably a late eighteenth century feature as no such opening is shown on Buck's East Prospect of 1741. The bell on the grass is probably from the tower.

The Old Gannock Gate (7)

The gate stood at the southern junction of Gannock Terrace and Goodwin's Road. The 'new road' referred to is what is now called London Road, created by the King's Lynn Paving Commissioners to bypass the long established but tortuous route into the centre of town via Southgate Street, Friar Street, All Saints Street, Bridge Street, and Church Street. The order to start construction was made on 13 June 1803 and on 28 July 1806 arrangements were put in hand to surface the completed road with Hardwick gravel.

The South Gate (8)

This is arguably Edwards's finest drawing The original was probably drawn around 1800. It certainly pre-dates 1817 when Edwards organised the construction of the footway through the eastern wing of the gate. The figures drawing water give a useful insight into the way Edwards's work evolved. In 1815 John Sell Cotman published a print of the South Gate

XV Drawing Water at the South Gate, Detail from a print drawn, etched and published by John Sell Cotman, 1815.

(dedicated to Edwards's close friend Daniel Gurney). This print shows nine people drawing water and those in **(8)** are all present. In view of the difficulty Edwards had with drawing people, it seems likely that his original South Gate sketch was devoid of figures, but when in the 1820's he produced his wash version, he borrowed three from Cotman's engraving.

The significance of the pail carriers is explained by Armes. "In South Lynn, at this period, quality was often manifested by the water pails as well as by the lanthorns. At this time South Lynn parish had no water from public works. All were supplied from the stream which, passing under the South Gates, empties itself into the Nar. East of the South Gates, through the inn yard, the boys and girls of South Lynn were to be seen always at low water, often quarrelling for a turn to stand upon the large stone from which they dipped the pail.

These pails, as I have said, indicated social position, thus: One pail of wood, specially if old, was extreme poor. Two good wooden pails and a pair of yokes, as they were called, moderately poor. Two good painted wood pails and yokes, moderately rich. Two tin pails painted, and a hoop, extreme rich. The girls, with these latter, of course kept aloof from the mere wooden pail party, and were understood to represent a higher order in society."**(XV)**.[35.]

Fragment of a Bellasis or Outwork (9)

This drawing represents a rare Edwards excursion into the post mediaeval period. The brick structure stood more-or-less where the small roundabout now manages the traffic to and from the South Gate. It seems to be the remains of the northern wing of a gatehouse which barred entry from the Hardwick Causeway to a Civil War outwork protecting the South Gate (note the iron gate pivot). Such an outwork is shown on Bell's Groundplat (c.1686) and its site is indicated on Rastrick's map of 1725. It appears to represent the only evidence for brick structures associated with the Civil War defences of the town.

B. CHURCHES, CHAPELS AND COLLEGES

Edwards's letter of appointment to the lectureship required him to preach a sermon on alternate Sundays in St. Margaret's Church and St. Nicholas Chapel. These were the two functioning mediaeval ecclesiastical buildings in the parish and naturally attracted his pen and brush, but there were also a number of other pre-Reformation ecclesiastical buildings which, though redundant, had survived the ravages of time through adaptation for new uses or as picturesque ruins. In addition, there were other such buildings demolished within his living memory, but before he took up drawing. Edwards produced drawings of most of them, although he does not seem to have recorded the mediaeval Trinity Chapel, attached to St. Margaret's Church, the demolition of which he, as a Paving Commissioner, was instrumental in achieving.

St. Margaret's Church (10)(11)(12)(13)(14)(15)(16)

Despite the central position of St. Margaret's church in his life, Edwards does not appear to have left a drawing of the whole building comparable to his fine view of St. Nicholas Chapel **(18)**. In selecting subjects for his Antiquities series, he only included the view of the church's east end. However when his daughter Ann copied that sketchbook for her husband, she substituted an unfinished drawing of St. Margaret's from the west for the section of the Red Mount Chapel and this drawing has been included at **(10)**.

The view of the east end **(11)** has scarcely changed. Only the central niche has been modified. This drawing was subsequently engraved by Sherman and published as a print by Day and Haghe.

XVI Lectern and figures. St Margaret's Church, King's Lynn.

The drawing of the lantern **(12)** is taken from Beloe's 'Our Borough : Our Churches.'[36.] It is not attributed to Edwards and the whereabouts of the original is unknown, but the caption is undoubtedly his. The lantern which surmounted the central tower of St. Margaret's was erected in the 1480's and was similar to the Octagon of Ely Cathedral, which dates from 1338 and may well have provided the model for the Lynn example.

The interior views (13) (14) are not from either sketchbook. Like all Edwards's work, they are unsigned, but their style is unmistakably his and (13) was published as an engraving by Day and Haghe, with the original sketch attributed to him. The framework of (13) remains much the same, although Bell's reredos was replaced in 1899, following the restoration of the chancel. The figures in the foreground, studying the brass of Robert Braunche, could well be John Britton and his wife (XVI). The other interior view (14) records the essentially Georgian character of the furnishings installed in the rebuilt nave following the destruction meted out by the great storm of 1741. These were all swept away in the 1870's gothic revival restoration of the nave, save for the pulpit, which was reduced in size and moved across the aisle to its present site.

The south aisle (lumber room) (15) has now been cleared and is the setting for the fine brasses of Robert Braunche and Adam de Walsoken. The grave slab of Walter Coney, visible in the foreground, was returned to the Trinity Chapel in 1898.

The Old Grammar School (17)

Originally built as the Charnel Chapel of St. John the upper chamber became the free grammar school in the reign of Henry VIII. The drawing presents some problems. Edwards went to school there between 1772 and 1778 and therefore, as a child, knew the building well, but it was demolished the year after he left, long before he attempted his reconstruction from memory, with the aid of prints by Bell and Buck. Unfortunately his memory let him down as to the building's siting. He shows it attached to the surviving western bay of the collapsed northern aisle of the church. Beloe convincingly shows this to be an error and states that "It was built at the westward corner clear of the church, and when the north aisle was widened its north-west corner was brought up to the east corner of the chapel. The first of the northern windows of the fifteenth - century aisle remains and would not have been inserted if the wall of the fourteenth - century chapel was there and blocked it."[37.]

In 1779 a shambles with schoolroom over was built on the site but this in turn was demolished in 1914. The site now forms part of the Saturday Market Place.

The Chapel of St. Nicholas (18)(19)

St. Nicholas Chapel is the building most associated with Edwards in his role as lecturer. He was buried there with his wife and eldest son. His historical account of the chapel concludes with "The whole chapel was new glazed, and otherwise completely repaired in the year 1805,"[38.] and the drawing probably dates from that time. This is one of his best works and is topographically accurate, save for the pathway which has been moved to the centre foreground from the far right for artistic reasons. The door (19) is still to be seen in the vestry although virtually all its decoration has worn off, making Edward's full colour record all the more significant.

The chapel looks much the same today save for the spire which was replaced in 1869-70 by one designed by George Gilbert Scott. The building was declared redundant in 1989 and is now in the care of The Churches Conservation Trust.

XVII South porch of St Nicholas Chapel, King's Lynn.
Engraved by Noble from a drawing by Mackensie for
The Architectural Antiquities of Great Britain. 1811.

The Chapel of the Virgin at Ladybridge (20)

This chapel stood where the small, painted roundabout is now situated at the junction of Stonegate Street, Church Street and Bridge Street. The western parapet of the bridge still survives. It bears the date 1792, marking a rebuilding in that year. On 11 June 1804, the Paving Commissioners agreed to purchase the old chapel from George Hawkins gentleman, of King's Lynn, for £350. A week later they approved a plan for the widening of the bridge including the removal of the chapel although fate played a part for William Richards records that in 1806 "there was a very high tide which demolished the remaining ruins of Our Lady's Chapel on the Bridge."[39.]

The Millfleet, from the Ladybridge to London Road, was filled in in 1897-8 making it difficult now to visualise a bridge or the chapel in the locality.

The Red Mount Chapel (21)(22)(23)(24)

Edwards was fascinated by the Red Mount Chapel. His historical account of the building concludes with ".....in 1783, the use of this chapel was granted to a teacher of navigation for an observatory. But at this period it received an injury, which must hasten its destruction. In order to ascend the roof, the north window was cut down, and made into a door-way. As the chapel already overhung its base, and was held together principally by the strength of the side walls, it was impossible that such an injudicious alteration could be made, without hazard to the whole fabrick. The opposite, or south wall, is now rent from the top to the bottom, and the joints of the beautiful vaulted roof are so much opened as to admit the wind and water, which must soon decay and destroy it. In the late

XVIII Red Mount Chapel, Lynn, Norfolk. Etched by Smith from a drawing by Rachel Gurney for The Architectural Antiquities of Great Britain. 1811.

mayoralty of George Edwards, Esq. the buttresses were carefully repaired; and it is hoped that, before it be too late, some further means will be resorted to for the preservation of this venerable and curious structure."[40.]

The earliest view (21) must be before 1808 for it shows the major dilapidations. The surrounding wall, shown in (22), is important to the understanding of the development of the building. Bell's Groundplat (c.1686) seems to show a wall, pierced by windows, surrounding the chapel and Rastrick's map (1725) shows the chapel surrounded by a crenellated wall, also pierced by windows. Buck's East Prospect (1741) shows the ruins of the wall much as they are in (22).

Curiously the section of the chapel (24) was the only piece of Edwards artwork to be used to illustrate his published historical account. The main engraving in the piece is from a drawing by his friend Rachel Gurney (XVIII).

The Workhouse formerly the Chapel of St. James (25)(26)

Armes refers to the workhouse in the following terms: "Of St. James's workhouse, which so lately fell of extreme old age, I only express my satisfaction that the poor have now a house so much more convenient, although to my mind, in the wrong locality, and, also, my regret that the ruin of St. James's has not been completely swept away, and an edifice of some sort erected on the site which should have been, architecturally, an ornament to the town."[41.]

He is referring to the fact that on 20 August 1854 the central tower (25) collapsed, killing a Mr. Andrews, who was repairing the clock and a pauper named Cana. The workhouse master and another man were buried alive in the rubble. The new St. James Workhouse was opened in 1856 in Extons Road.

A small section of the north transept and one other fragment of the old chapel survive, but the site is now occupied by the London Road Methodist Church Hall and Vancouver House, a building which one suspects Armes would not have thought an 'ornament to the town.'

The four beds framed by the great gothic arch (26) encapsulate in a poignant way the original and later function of this building.

Thoresby College (27)

Edwards featured a drawing of Thoresby College in his Scraps and Demolitions series, but since the dismemberment of that sketchbook it has disappeared. As its associated historical note survives, a substitute drawing has been provided to stand with it. The drawing is by William Taylor, a close friend of Edwards. He made copies of many drawings, including several by Edwards. It is just possible that this is a copy of the missing drawing, but the text reference to sash windows makes that unlikely.

After the college's dissolution in 1547, the building was granted to the corporation who sold it on to the Town Clerk, Robert Houghton.

Since then it has had a variety of uses: dwellinghouse, private school, mineral water factory, but in 1963 it was bought by Ruth Lady Fermoy and her daughter Mrs Shand-Kydd and presented to the King's Lynn Preservation Trust for restoration. It is now the headquarters of the Trust and accommodates a youth hostel, Citizens Advice Bureau, a number of flats, and the great hall, which is available for public hire.

C. FRIARIES

The remains of four friaries existed in Edwards time; those of the Franciscans (Greyfriars), Carmelites (Whitefriars), Dominicans (Blackfriars) and the Austins. He was to witness further destruction of these remains, but not before making a record.

The Greyfriars (28)(29)

Edwards's original pencil sketch of the Greyfriars tower is in the Norfolk Record Office (**XI**).[42.] It is initialled EE and dated 1808, being drawn shortly after the central arch was opened up by his brother George, in his mayoralty. It is the only pencil drawing of a Lynn subject by him to have been identified in a public collection and is valuable in demonstrating the progress of his work from pencil drawing to engraving, and onward to the wash version .

The pencil drawing is devoid of anything living, but when in 1809 J. Stewart engraved it for Britton's Beauties, he introduced two people and three cattle, presumably to give the picture life and scale (**XIX**). Edwards, in turn, when completing his wash version in the 1820's, included two of Stewart's cattle in a similar sequence of events to that described under the South Gate (**8**).

The building featured between the tower and St. Margaret's Church is Tower House, Edwards's family home. It was subsequently used as a hostel for assistants at Jermyn's, a High Street store, but has long since been demolished.

The gateway (**29**) stood at the junction of St. James Street and Tower Place, on the roadway that now fronts the bingo hall. After demolition by the Paving Commissioners, Edwards bought two tons of cobbles from the site for his own use.

XIX Tower of the Grey Friars Monsastery, Lynn, Norfolk. Engraved by J. Stewart from a drawing by Edwards for The Beauties of England and Wales. 1809.

The Gate of the Whitefriars (30)

Nothing survives in this view except for the gate itself, the necessary consolidation of which has inevitably left it devoid of much of its earlier charm. The masts are a reminder of the former importance of the River Nar for shipping, especially whaling. The comment about Mr. Valinger provides a warning about taking buildings built of early brick at face value for reclaimed building material from the friaries was used extensively in the town after the dissolution.

The Gate of St. Augustine's Monastery (31)

The gateway survives in Austin Street much as Edwards depicts it. It now forms part of the perimeter wall of the Borough Council Offices.

Monastery of the Dominicans (32)

The wall shown in this drawing is the western wall of the friary cloister. It stood between Market Street and Blackfriars Street, largely on the site of the present telephone exchange. Between 1850 and 1852 the remaining ruins of this friary were demolished to clear the site for redevelopment. At that time, the elder Beloe saved a large stone cross which now stands beneath the Greyfriars Tower.

D. ALMSHOUSES

In 1843 the Commissioners enquiring into public charities reported on those in King's Lynn. The report mentions five almshouses, viz. the Hospital of St. Mary Magdalen, in Gaywood, St. James's Hospital or Bedehouses, Framingham's Hospital, the Wesleyan or Smith's Almshouses, and Valinger's Almshouse in South Lynn. All but the first have been demolished so it is fortunate that Edwards decided to record two of these, both dating from the seventeenth century. Since his time benefactors have endowed several more almshouses and they continue to perform a useful role in the town.

The Broad Street Almshouse (33)

This almshouse was incorporated under the name 'The Master and Brethren of the Hospital of Framingham' after the man, whose legacy of £1,000, enabled it to be completed and endowed. Ten poor men were accommodated, one of whom was to be chosen as a master to read divine service, twice daily.

It stood in Paradise Garden, to the east of Broad Street, on land granted by the corporation.

The site is now the Vancouver Centre service yard. In 1845, the corporation decided to extend the cattle market. This required the relocation of this almshouse. The new site chosen was the corporation depot opposite the Millfleet, between the Broad Walk and the Gaywood River. The new building was opened in 1848 and still flourishes today.

The Bede House (34)

The Bede House stood on the west side of St. James Road, more-or-less on the site of the police station yard. This drawing pre-dates 1822 for, in that year, the almshouse was rebuilt, utilising the legacy of Benjamin Smith with assistance from the corporation. The date stone, inscribed Thomas Soame, Mayor 1630, together with the town arms, was salvaged and set in the gable of the new building which itself was demolished in the early 1950's to make way for the police station.

E. PUBLIC BUILDINGS

This section groups together drawings of a number of buildings which had some measure of public use.

The Guildhall (35)

This view of the former Trinity Guildhall looks much the same today as it did then. The only real difference is that the Lynn Arms public house, featured on the extreme left of the picture, was demolished to make way for the late Victorian town hall extension. In his various public roles, Edwards was a frequent visitor to the Guildhall. The mayoral procession, preceded by the staff, mace and sword bearers, is heading towards St. Margaret's Church to take part in a civic service.

The building is still in civic and public use and houses heritage attractions including the town's regalia.

St. George's Hall (36)

Edwards executed this drawing on 7 June 1826, but the viewpoint he has chosen could not have been gained at that time for the north elevation of the Hall was and still is obscured by the buildings of the adjacent Shakespeare public house. What Edwards has done is attempt to disentangle the Guildhall from its surroundings, but in so doing he has inadvertently omitted the central bay. In 1861 Henry Baines, who clearly had access to Edwards's drawing or a copy thereof, produced a version with the missing bay restored (**XX**).

In 1826 the building was purchased by the Everard family from the estate of William Lee Warner. Perhaps this is what prompted Edwards to produce his drawing. The Everards used the building as a wool warehouse. In 1920 it was sold

XX St. George's Guildhall from a sketch by the Rev. Edward Edwards. Drawing by Henry Baines. 29 March 1861.

to G.M. Bridges & Son Ltd., scenic artists, but by 1945 it was derelict and under threat of demolition for the expansion of the nearby garage. It was saved by Alexander Penrose and converted into an arts centre. Queen Elizabeth (later to be the Queen Mother) opened it in July 1951 as part of the inaugural King's Lynn Festival. The Guildhall is now owned by the National Trust and, as a theatre and cinema, still plays a useful role in the life of the town.

The Tuesday Market Place Crosses (37)(38)

Edwards had access to an engraving of the Tuesday Market Place by Henry Bell, an earlier version of the more well known one of c.1686 (**XXI**). From this he extracted the market cross and made it the subject of a separate drawing (**37**). This cross was replaced in 1707-10 by one designed by Bell (**38**). There are many engravings of this cross so the drawing by Edwards would be unremarkable were it not for the fact that he is recording its demolition.

XXI Tuesday Market Place, King's Lynn. Engraving by Henry Bell. c1686

The latin inscription translates as, 'This market colonnade, together with the provision markets placed on both sides, and the fish market at the rear, was brought forward entirely at the costs of gentlemen from the county as well as inhabitants of the town, for public use and ornament. Let it be said that this work, begun under the auspices of Charles Turner Mayor in the year 1707, was finished by John Berney, Mayor in 1710. By Henry Bell, architect.'

The building material removed in the demolition was taken to Hillington Park and is believed to be the stone used to construct the main gateway.

The Old Custom House and Mr. Sommersby's House (39)

This is another view taken from Bell's engraving. The house of Mr. Sommersby, Edwards's grandfather, is to the right. This was replaced in the late eighteenth century by a building which is now a solicitor's office.

With the custom officers moving to the building on Purfleet Quay, now called the Custom House, the old Custom House was demolished (c.1703) to make way for a new mansion for merchant Charles Turner. An inn called the Angel was later built between the mansion and Mr. Sommersby's house.

Turner's house burned down in 1768 and was replaced by the present bank building which was refronted in the 1950s. The Angel Inn in turn was demolished to make way for the new Market House opened in 1832 to replace the demolished market cross (38) and shambles. Twenty-four years later, the market house was replaced by the corn exchange.

F. HOUSES AND HALLS

Before the early nineteenth century work of the Paving Commissioners radically changed the whole look of the town many of Lynn's streets were 'timber framed' in character. With the objective of straightening and widening the streets, the Commissioners laid plans for the removal of prominent projections and overhangs, many of which were the jettied upper storeys of timber framed buildings. Several of today's brown brick facades hide the remains of such buildings, especially in the High Street. This being the case, it is a little surprising that Edwards did not draw more of them before they disappeared. He did, however, leave drawings of two of the most important examples, Coney's House and the Greenland Fishery as well as an animated sketch of demolition in progress in King Street.

House in Bridge Street (40)

Edwards's commentary bears testimony to his rigorous approach to historical evidence. However, it is now generally accepted that the house was built for merchant John Atkin in 1605. (The wall paintings Edwards refers to bear the date 1612 and the initials J.A.).

The building is now known as the 'Greenland Fishery' but this name has only applied to the whole since 1912 when the younger Beloe established his Greenland Fishery Museum there. Edwards does not use the name, confirming that it did not apply to the whole building in his day. Some time in its history it became divided with the southern portion being run as an inn under the name 'The Waterman's Arms.' With it becoming a popular haunt of the Nar based whalers, its name was changed to the 'Greenland Fishery Inn' in 1796.

By Beloe's time, the wall paintings had once more been covered and were not to see the light of day again until the removal of five layers of wallpaper during restoration work in the late 1940s.

Beloe's museum contained an interesting and varied collection of largely local exhibits, including all the drawings from Edwards's Antiquities series and thirteen of those from the Scraps and Demolitions. Most were framed for display and reproductions of some were sold as postcards.

Unfortunately on 12 June 1941 the building suffered severe bomb damage, although this was largely confined to the rear. The exhibits were transferred to the Town Museum and the building, owned since 1933 by the Norfolk Archaeological Trust, was repaired. In 1997 ownership of the whole property passed to the King's Lynn Preservation Trust.

A typescript inventory of the drawings transferred to the Town Museum in the 1940s lists this piece as, 'Greenland Fishery 1803,' giving a date which, although reasonable, does not appear on the drawing itself.

Cony's House (41)

This ornate timber-framed building stood on the eastern corner of the High Street/Saturday Market Place and clearly caught Edwards's eye long before its demolition in 1816. During his early years as lecturer, it was owned by brazier John Coward. Hillen records that in 1787 the churchwardens (of St. Margaret's) sold him brass weighing 10 stone at 5 pence per 1lb.[43.] Perhaps it was Coward who in 1804 also bought the stolen brasses from sexton and gravedigger William Willblood, referred to by Edwards under (16).

Coward's widow sold the house to the builder and Paving Commissioners surveyor, Samuel Newham, who had plans to demolish and redevelop the site. At the time the Commissioners were prepared to pay for land given up for street widening when replacement buildings were set back. In March 1816 Newham offered to sell them 58 ½ square feet of ground for £60. Thinking his demand "most exorbitant," they suggested a sum of 20 guineas, which he in turn rejected. The demolition did take place, however, and the replacement building, which occupies the site today, features the Commissioners' characteristic rounded corner. During much of the 19th century and into the 1920's, the building was occupied by the office of Mr. Thew's Lynn Advertiser.

William Armes adds colour to these events by describing his schoolboy involvement with 'Old Cunard' as he calls John Coward. After making reference to juvenile gambling, he recalled, "No boy, however, became richer by this process, as all was expended in tamarinds from Gresenwaites, cakes from Hilyard's or peablowers, arrow heads and sundry other matters of lead and tin from 'old Cunard's,' as we were wont to call the worthy who then held possession of Walter Coney's house, at what we should now call Thew's corner. I have frequently been one of a school deputation to wait upon the said 'Old Cunard,' and in the upper room of that old house (used as a workshop) have often waited while the worthy man hammered out for us sundry articles required for the school. Doubtless, the bustling intelligence of the newspaper office, as compared with the blows and knocks of the aforesaid worker in brass and iron, is indicative of an advancing age. But, I confess that I could sit with Mr. Taylor at my old window over the Shambles and lament the loss of that quaint old house whose successor (I beg pardon of Mr. Thew) is so entirely unworthy of its ancestor."[44]

The said William Taylor published engravings of the building and many of the carved timbers from its facades in his Antiquities of Lynn.[45]

House in King Street (42)

With this view one can readily imagine Edwards coming across the demolition work in progress and hurrying home to fetch his sketchbook and pencil.

The timber-framed building was replaced by one with a brown brick facade and an arched access to Aickman's Yard. Being an ironfounder, John Aickman cast a large plaque to commemorate his 1827 redevelopment of the site. It is still to be seen over the archway (**XXII**).

XXII Plaque over the archway to Aickman's Yard, King's Lynn.

The building and railings to the right (the former girl's High School) are little changed today.

Ancient Hall now the Tailor's Arms (43)(44)

This building stood on the site of what is now the Town House Museum on the west side of Queen Street, opposite Thoresby College. Its origin and purpose are no clearer today than they were to Edwards in 1833.

In 1654 the public house was "late the Cross Keys now the Swan." In 1723 it was the Black Swan, but in 1742 it was described as the "Taylor's Arms, formerly the Black Swan since the Stockholm." It seems to have come into the Taylor family, via the marriage of Alice Holley to Simon Taylor, the inn sign being Taylor's coat of arms. However, the origin of the name soon became forgotten and by 1836 it was being spelt 'Tailor's'.

A copy of this drawing by William Taylor has pencilled on it "Demolished 1905."

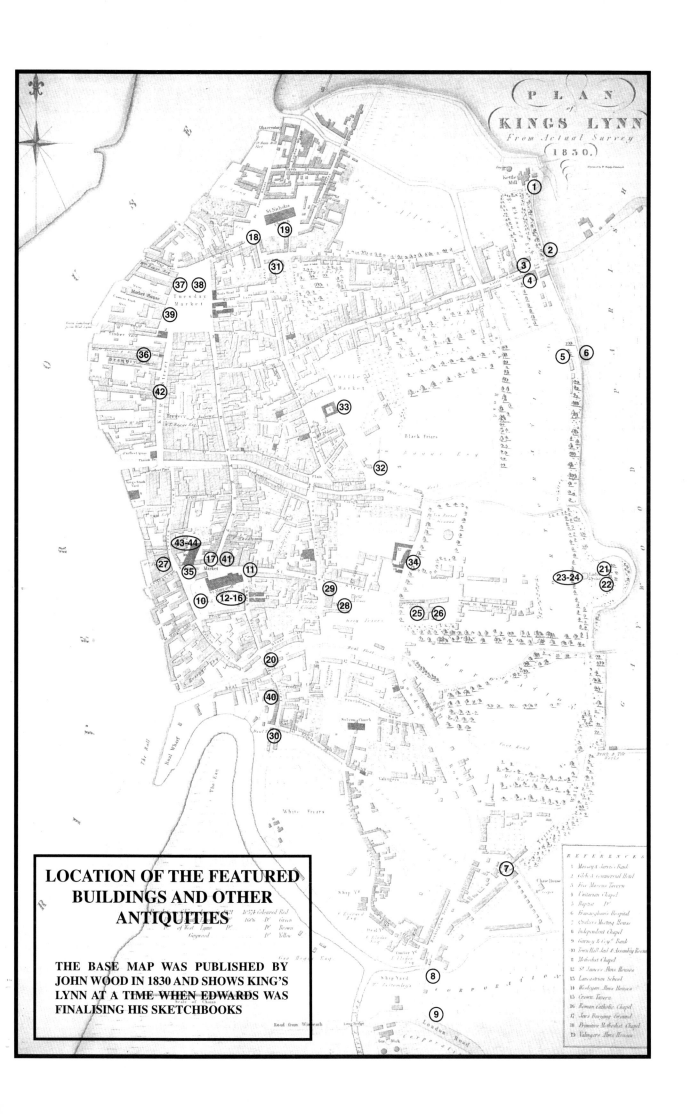

LOCATION OF THE FEATURED BUILDINGS AND OTHER ANTIQUITIES

THE BASE MAP WAS PUBLISHED BY JOHN WOOD IN 1830 AND SHOWS KING'S LYNN AT A TIME WHEN EDWARDS WAS FINALISING HIS SKETCHBOOKS

NOTES AND REFERENCES

1. Lynn Advertiser 21 March 1849.

2. Details of Edwards's immediate ancestry are contained in a document entitled 'Genealogical Memoranda from my Uncle, related 28 Feb 1802.' It was compiled by his brother, John, from a conversation with their uncle Nicholas. All the quoted extracts in this section are from this document. King's Lynn Museum. (KLM), KL.209.976.

3. Edwards recorded the key events of his life in a document entitled 'VITA BREVIS,' a typescript copy of which is in the King's Lynn Museum. KLM. Edwards Personal File.

4. In 1966 this cup was in the possession of Miss D. Edwards of Auckland, New Zealand. There is a black and white snapshot of it in the King's Lynn Museum. It bears the inscriptions 'EDWARD EDWARDS AB 1787' and 'CCCC Philosophia Premium.' KLM Edwards Personal File.

5. King's Lynn Borough Archives (KLBA). KL/C7/15. fol 80.

6. Thew. P16. A number of Edward's sermons were published including one entitled 'The Progress of Evil,' preached shortly after the death of Robert Robinson, aged 19, who was shot on 11 December 1821 in the act of robbing a shop in the High Street.

7. Katharine Fry's Book. P22. Edward's friendship with the Gurneys is also covered in the 'Memoirs of Rachel Gurney'. Norfolk Record Office (NRO) MC 1627/1

8. History, Gazetteer, and Directory of Norfolk by William White. 1836. P472.

9. The inkstand is in the Mayor's Parlour, Town Hall, King's Lynn. It bears the inscription 'TO THE REVEREND EDWARD EDWARDS M.A., F.S.A. THIS TRIBUTE OF ESTEEM IS PRESENTED In united testimony of a grateful sense of the zeal & ability with which he has for more than half a century discharged the sacred duties of his office as LECTURER OF KING'S LYNN. 1842.'

10. Letter. KLM. KL209. 976.

11. NRO BLII c/27.

12. Hankinson. PP233-4.

13. Lynn Advertiser 21 March 1849.

14. The quoted passages in this section are from a collection of ten letters, typescripts of which are in the King's Lynn Museum. They were sent to George and Ann Munford by Edwards and his children between 2 June and 13 August 1830 as they travelled through Belgium, Germany, Switzerland, Italy and France. KLM Edwards Personal File.

15. Lynn Advertiser 21 March 1849.

16. Letter 4. 22 June 1830 from Karlsruhe. KLM Edwards Personal File.

17. Minutes of the Society of Antiquaries. His certificate of election has not survived.

18. Britton's Architectural Antiquities Vol.II.

19. Britton's Architectural Antiquities. Vol.III. P61.

20. PCC WILLS PROB11/2091. Edward Edwards 1849.

21. A typescript list entitled 'The Merchants of Lynn. Extra illustrations' is in the Bradfer Lawrence Collection in the NRO. It post dates 1941 and includes the following:- '68 South Gates, Lynn, an original pencil sketch by Rev. E Edwards, ditto looking NE, 80 Lynn from the West, pencil sketch by Rev. E Edwards, 81 Gaywood Church from Gaywood Hall Moat by ditto, 179 Pencil sketch of Lynn Harbour looking North may 24 (18)09 by Edwards,' but none of these can be identified in the collection. NRO BL/ VI a (VII)

22. The details of this distribution are given on the flyleaf.

23. PCC Will PROB11/2091. Each was to choose one item or set by turns according to their ages, first agreeing what were to be deemed sets.

24. KLM KL.494.991.

25. The statement is written on a loose sheet which was probably the sketchbook's flyleaf. It reads, 'The last of these drawings, which have afforded occasional amusement for upwards of twenty years, was pasted in Nov.20 1828 by E. Edwards.' The following comment is also written on this sheet, "found under Edwards drawing of S Gates when cleaned & renovated April 1967 by J. Skillen 61 Glebe Place SW3." KLM Edwards Personal File.

26. Drawing (43) Ancient Hall now the Tailor's Arms.

27. Suffolk Record Office. R164/44.

28. It is clear that Beloe had recently acquired the drawings for he labours the point with comments such as 'whose sketches I possess' (P.78), 'I have the original sketch of it by E. Edwards' (P.103). 'They are all in my possession' (P.106) and 'Among the drawings and sketches of the Rev. E. Edwards which are now with

me,.....' (P.190).

29. The Merchants of Lynn. In the event none of the drawings were used for that purpose.
30. NRO BLII c/27.
31. Armes, P57-58.
32. KLBA KL/C7/15. fol 211
33. KLBA KL/C7/15. fol 214.
34. Armes, P4
35. Armes, P41-42
36. Beloe, Plate 20 Facing page 96.
37. Beloe, page 79.
38. Rev. Edward Edwards, F.S.A. Some Account of the Chapel of St. Nicholas at King's Lynn, Norfolk. The Architectural Antiquities Vol III P57-60.
39. Richards, W. P1213.
40. Rev. Edward Edwards, F.S.A. Some Account of The Chapel of our Lady on the Mount or Red Mount at Lynn Norfolk. The Architectural Antiquities Vol III P61-66.
41. Armes, P18
42. NRO BL VI a (VII)
43. Hillen, P.387.
44. Armes, P20-21.
45. Taylor, W. 1844.

SELECT BIBLIOGRAPHY

Armes, W. Memories of Lynn. Papers read 1858 and published in the Lynn Advertiser 1872. Republished in 1990 by the Friends of the King's Lynn Local History Library.

Auker, R.H. Ancient Lynn, 1766-1848. King's Lynn (1977).

Beloe, E.M. Our Borough: Our Churches. Cambridge. 1899.

Bradfer-Lawrence, H.L. The Merchants of Lynn. In Ingleby's Supplement to Blomefield's Norfolk. 1929. pp.145-203.

Britton, J. The Architectural Antiquities of Great Britain, 5 vols. London. 1807-1826.

Clarke, H. and Carter, A. Excavations in King's Lynn 1963-1970. London. 1977.

Hankinson. Sketch of the Life of Thomas Edwards Hankinson M.A. 2 vols. Norwich. 1861.

Harrod, H. Report on the Deeds & Records of the Borough of King's Lynn. King's Lynn. 1874.

Hillen, H.J. The History of King's Lynn, Norfolk. 1907.

Mackerell, B. The History and Antiquities of King's Lynn. Norwich. 1738.

Owen, D.M. The Making of King's Lynn. London. 1984.

Parker, V. The Making of King's Lynn. Phillimore. 1971.

Parkin, C. The Topography of Freebridge Hundred and Half in the County of Norfolk. King's Lynn. 1762.

Richards, P. King's Lynn. Phillimore. 1990.

Richards, W. History of Lynn. 2 vols. King's Lynn. 1812.

Taylor, W. The Antiquities of King's Lynn, Norfolk. King's Lynn. 1844.

Thew, J. Dyker. Personal Recollections by a Lynn Sexagenarian. King's Lynn. 1891.

The Town Scene : Selected Topographical material from the King's Lynn Borough Collection. Souvenir Exhibition Catalogue 1973.

Vansittart, J. (Ed) Katherine Fry's Book. 1966.